AUDIO INCLUDED

Developing

Artist

PIANO LITERATURE BOOK 3

ORIGINAL KEYBOARD CLASSICS

REVISED EDITION

 ediate

Compiled and edited by

Nancy and Randall Faber

with Joanne Smith

Production Coordinator: Jon Ophoff
Cover: Terpstra Design, San Francisco
Engraving: Dovetree Productions, Inc.

FABER
PIANO ADVENTURES®

3042 Creek Drive
Ann Arbor, Michigan 48108

TABLE OF CONTENTS

The Periods of Music History 4

BAROQUE (1600–1750)

Krieger, Johann (1651–1735)
Minuet in A Minor 6

Duncombe, William (18th century)
Fanfare in C Major 8

Lully, Jean-Baptiste (1632–1687)
Minuet in D Minor 9

Anna Magdalena Bach Notebook

Musette in D Major (composer unknown) 10
Minuet in G Major (composer unknown) 12
Minuet in G Minor (Pezold, 1677–1733) 14
March in D Major (C.P.E. Bach, 1714–1788) 16

CLASSICAL (1750–circa 1830)

Bach, Johann Christoph Friedrich (1732–1795)
Solfeggio in D Major 18

Gossec, Francois (1734–1829)
Tambourin 20

Haslinger, Tobias (1787–1842)
Sonatina in C Major 22

Haydn, Franz Joseph (1732–1809)
German Dance in D Major 26
Minuet in G Major 27
Allegro in F Major 28

Clementi, Muzio (1752–1832)
Sonatina in C Major (Op. 36, No. 1) 30

Diabelli, Anton (1781–1858)
Sonatina in G Major, 1st Movement (Op. 168, No. 2) 37
Rondo for Four Hands (Op. 163, No. 6) 40

Beethoven, Ludwig van (1770–1827)
Two German Dances 46

Mozart, Leopold (1719–1787)
Allegro in A Major 48

ROMANTIC (circa 1830–1910)

Gurlitt, Cornelius (1820–1901)

A Little Flower (Op. 205, No. 11) 50

Burgmüller, Johann Friedrich (1806–1874)

Arabesque (Op. 100, No. 2) 52

Ballade (Op. 100, No. 15) 54

Harmony of the Angels (Op. 100, No. 21) 57

Schumann, Robert (1810–1856)

Wild Rider (Op. 68, No. 8) 60

Melody (Op. 68, No. 1) 62

Ellmenreich, Albert (1816–1905)

Spinning Song (Op. 14, No. 4) 64

Heller, Stephen (1813–1888)

Avalanche (Op. 45, No. 2) 67

Reinecke, Carl (1824–1910)

Gavotte (from Op. 183, No. 1) 70

CONTEMPORARY (circa 1900–present)

Rebikov, Vladimir (1866–1920)

Chinese Figurine (from *Christmas Gifts*, No. 13) 72

Playing Soldiers (Op. 31, No. 4) 74

Faber, Nancy (b. 1955)

The Moons of Jupiter 76

McKay, George Frederick (1899–1970)

Song of the Range Rider (from *Sagebrush Country*, No. 1) 78

Cowboy Song (from *Sagebrush Country*, No. 9) 80

Jacoby, Russell (b. 1955)

Sonatina 82

Alphabetical Index of Titles 85

Dictionary of Musical Terms 86

Audio Track Index 88

THE PERIODS OF MUSIC HISTORY

BAROQUE: 1600 – 1750

The term "Baroque" is used to describe the highly decorative style of art and architecture of the 17th century. It was an era of grandeur—of glittering royal courts in Europe, elaborate clothing, and wigs on men.

Music of the Baroque period was often highly ornate. Melodic lines were ornamented with trills or other embellishments. The Baroque period is also known for its use of counterpoint. Counterpoint ("note against note") is the technique of interweaving two or more melodic lines that imitate and support each other.

For most of this period the harpsichord, clavichord, and organ were the keyboard instruments used. The piano was not invented until about 1730.

CLASSICAL: 1750 – circa 1830

The Classical period was a time of two major revolutions: the American Revolution in 1776, and the French Revolution in 1789. Though the revolutions marked the rise of the middle class, men of the aristocracy still wore wigs and lace on formal occasions. Women curtsied and men bowed as they politely danced the minuet.

Composers of the Classical period preferred music that was charming and entertaining. They sought a return to simplicity and to what is "natural." Music of the period was elegant and melodic, avoiding counterpoint and using ornaments sparingly. "Taste" was very important, with purity and clarity as key elements of composition.

Haydn, Mozart, and Beethoven were the major composers of the Classical period. (Much of Beethoven's late work, however, ushered in the Romantic period.) These composers from Vienna were the creators of the piano sonata, the string quartet, and the orchestral symphony.

The keyboard instrument of this period was an early version of the piano called the fortepiano. The fortepiano was a rather delicate instrument with a light, clear tone. By the time Beethoven was an adult, however, the piano had increased in size, strength, and keyboard range. Now called the pianoforte, the instrument's power and dramatic capabilities made it an ideal instrument for the emerging Romantic period.

Romantic: circa 1830–1910

The Romantic period in music, art, and literature coincided with the rapid growth of industrial manufacturing in Europe and America, and with the westward expansion of the United States. It was also the time of America's Civil War and Queen Victoria's reign over the British Empire.

Music became openly emotional, and personal expression became more important than "taste" or pleasing an audience. With imagination and inspiration, composers often based their music on legends, folk songs, and fanciful tales of romance.

Orchestras increased in size and symphonic works became long and dramatic. The concerto (a composition for soloist and orchestra) became a work of technical display, designed to showcase a virtuoso soloist.

The 19th century may be considered the high point for piano music. The solo piano recital was popular in public concerts and in the private homes of the wealthy. With shadings of touch and pedal, the piano offered intense personal expression. Rubato—a flexible "give and take" in the rhythm—contributed to the emotional power of music and became a hallmark of the Romantic style.

Contemporary: circa 1900 – present

This century has been called the Age of Extremes. It has been dominated by two world wars (1914–1918 and 1939–1945), the Great Depression, and the breakup of both the British and Soviet Empires. It has also been a time of extraordinary technological advance. New forms of communication and travel staggered the imagination: telephone, radio, phonograph, motion pictures, television, the computer, automobiles, aircraft, and even spaceships!

Percussive effects, changing time signatures, abrupt rhythms, and dramatic contrasts are characteristic of modern music. Dissonance and extreme chromatic writing led to atonality (music having no key).

Experimentation has been a powerful force in 20th century music composition. Improvisation and such novel effects as plucking strings inside the piano have also added to the excitement and variety of contemporary piano music.

Minuet in A Minor

Johann Krieger
(1651–1735)

*The staccato marks indicate a slight detachment of the notes, characteristic of the Baroque style.

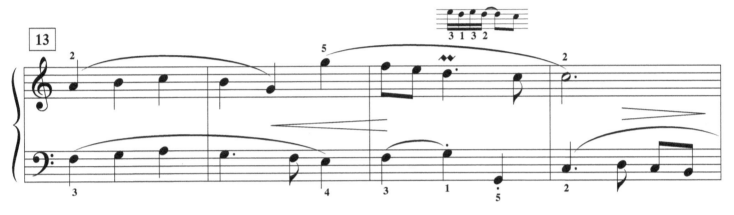

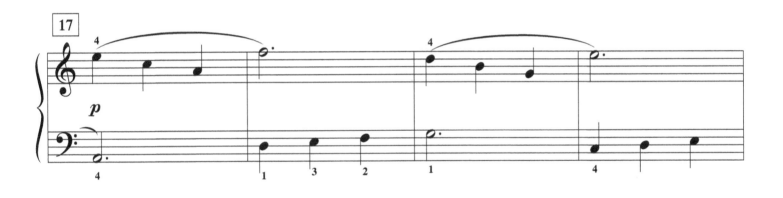

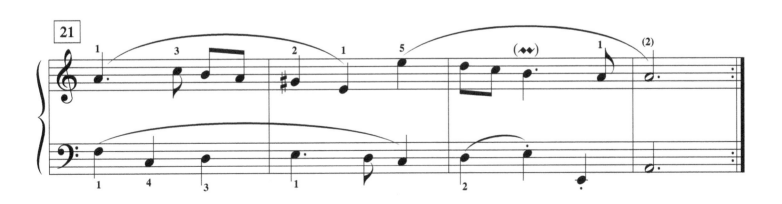

Fanfare in C Major

William Duncombe
(18th century)

Minuet in D Minor

Jean-Baptiste Lully
(1632–1687)

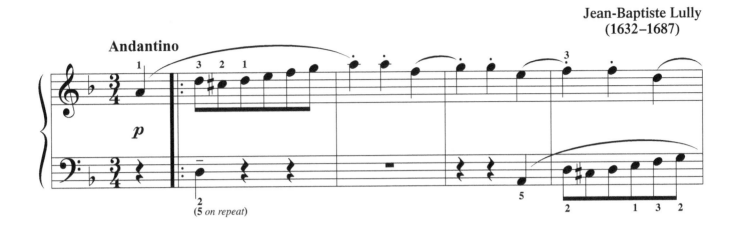

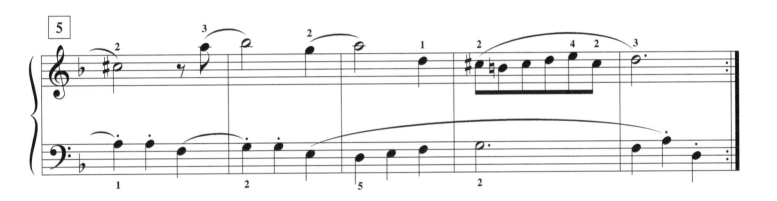

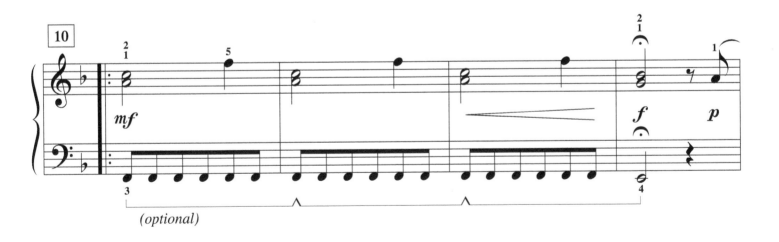

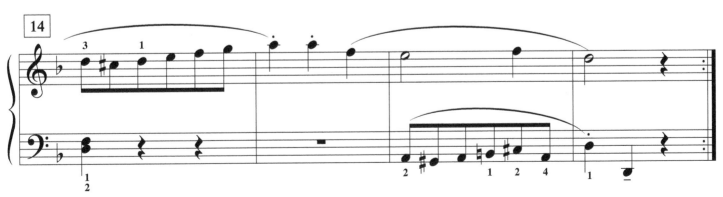

Musette in D Major
(from the *Notebook for Anna Magdalena Bach*)

Composer unknown

Allegretto

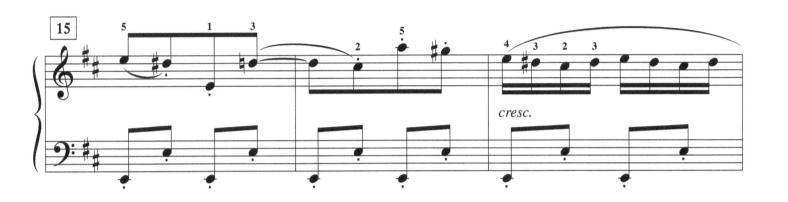

Minuet in G Major
(from the *Notebook for Anna Magdalena Bach*)

Composer unknown

*Unarticulated quarter notes may be played legato or non-legato.

*The manuscript is unclear whether this note should be D♮ or D♯.

Minuet in G Minor
(from the *Notebook for Anna Magdalena Bach*)

Christian Pezold
(1677–1733)

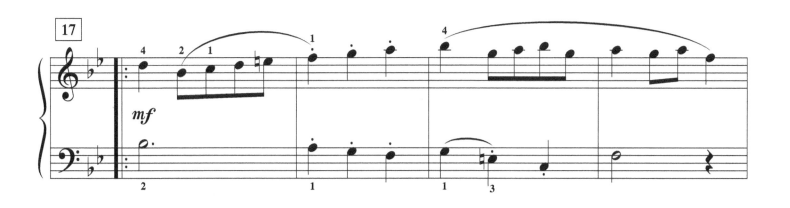

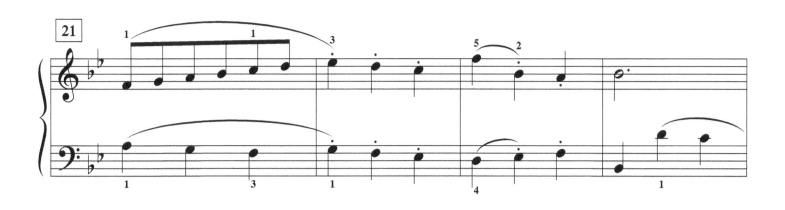

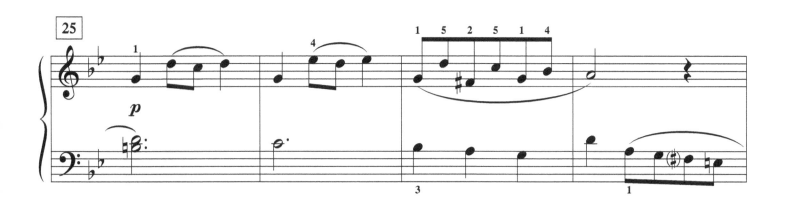

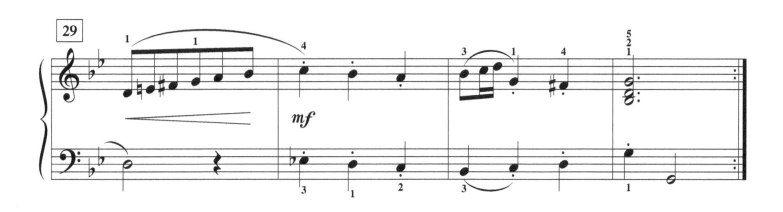

March in D Major
(from the *Notebook for Anna Magdalena Bach*)

Carl Philipp Emanuel Bach
(1714–1788)

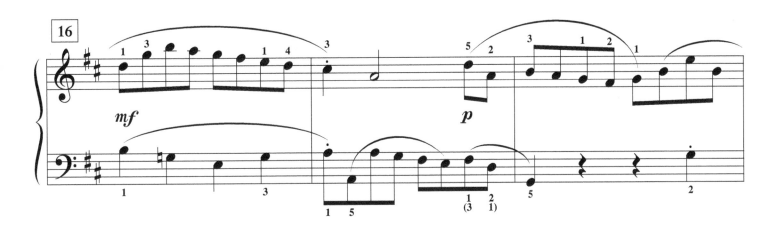

CLASSICAL
1750 - circa 1830

Solfeggio in D Major

Johann Christoph Friedrich Bach
(1732–1795)

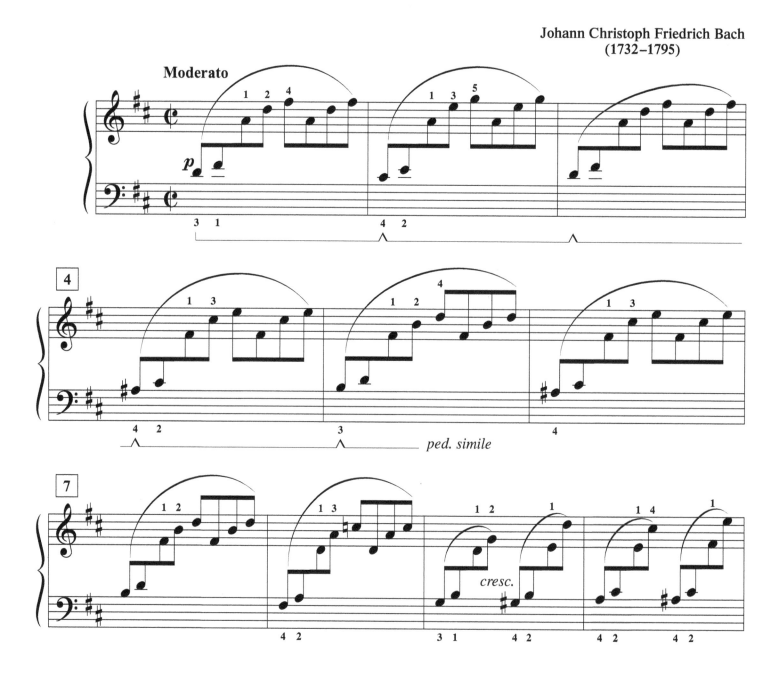

Tambourin

Francois Gossec
(1734–1829)

Sonatina in C Major

Tobias Haslinger
(1787–1842)

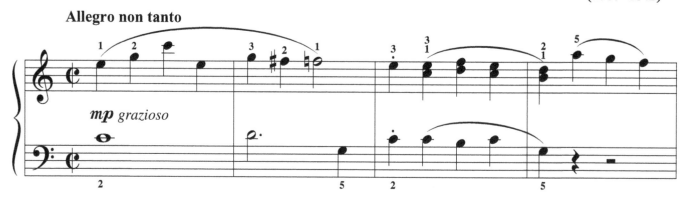

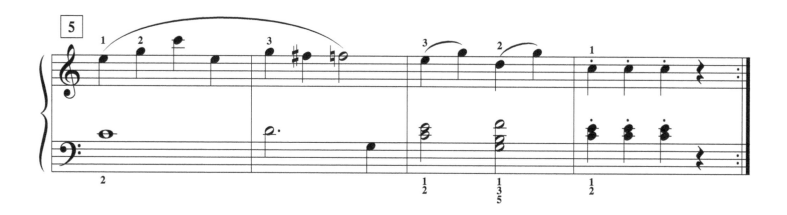

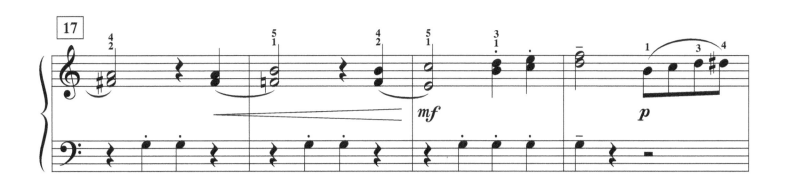

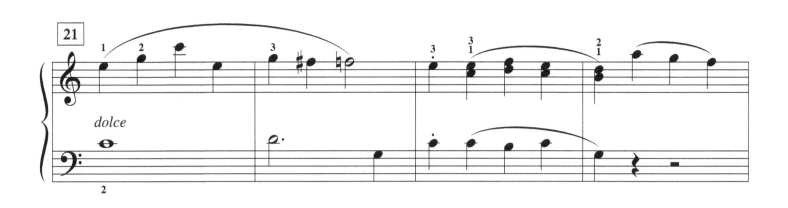

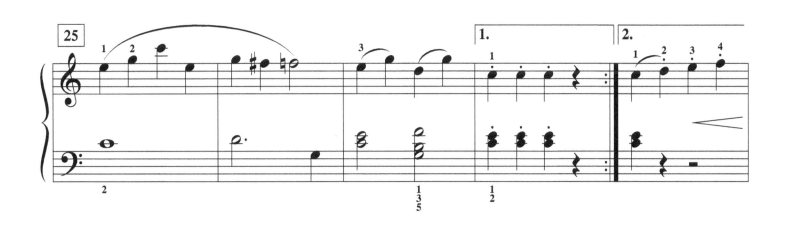

German Dance in D Major

Franz Joseph Haydn
(1732–1809)

Minuet in G Major

Franz Joseph Haydn
(1732–1809)

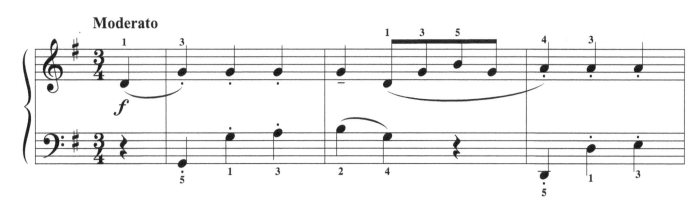

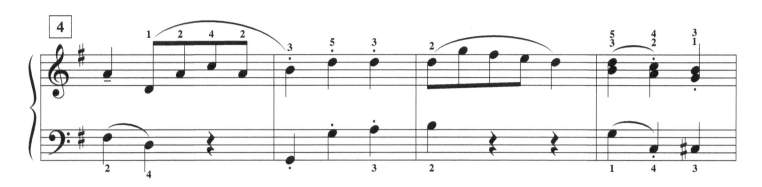

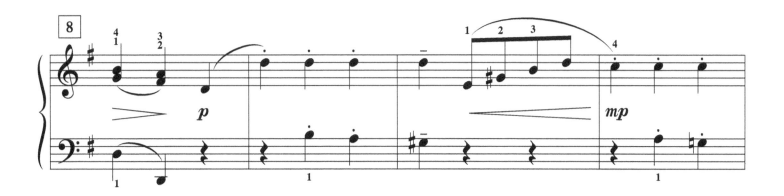

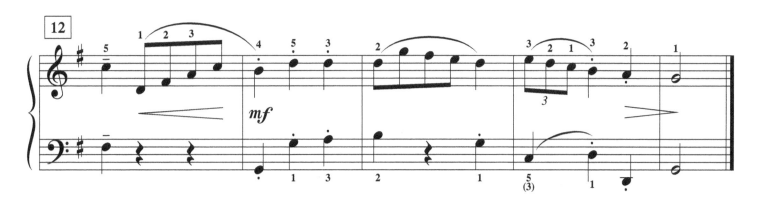

Allegro in F Major

Franz Joseph Haydn
(1732–1809)

Sonatina in C Major
(Opus 36, No. 1)

Muzio Clementi
(1752–1832)

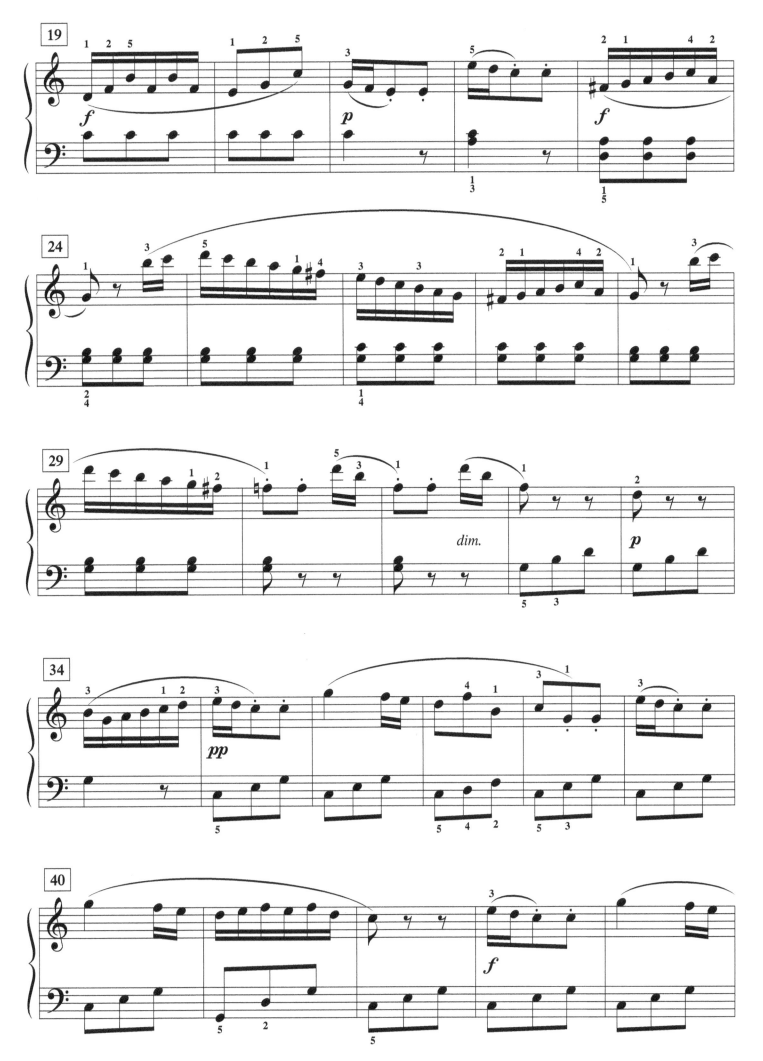

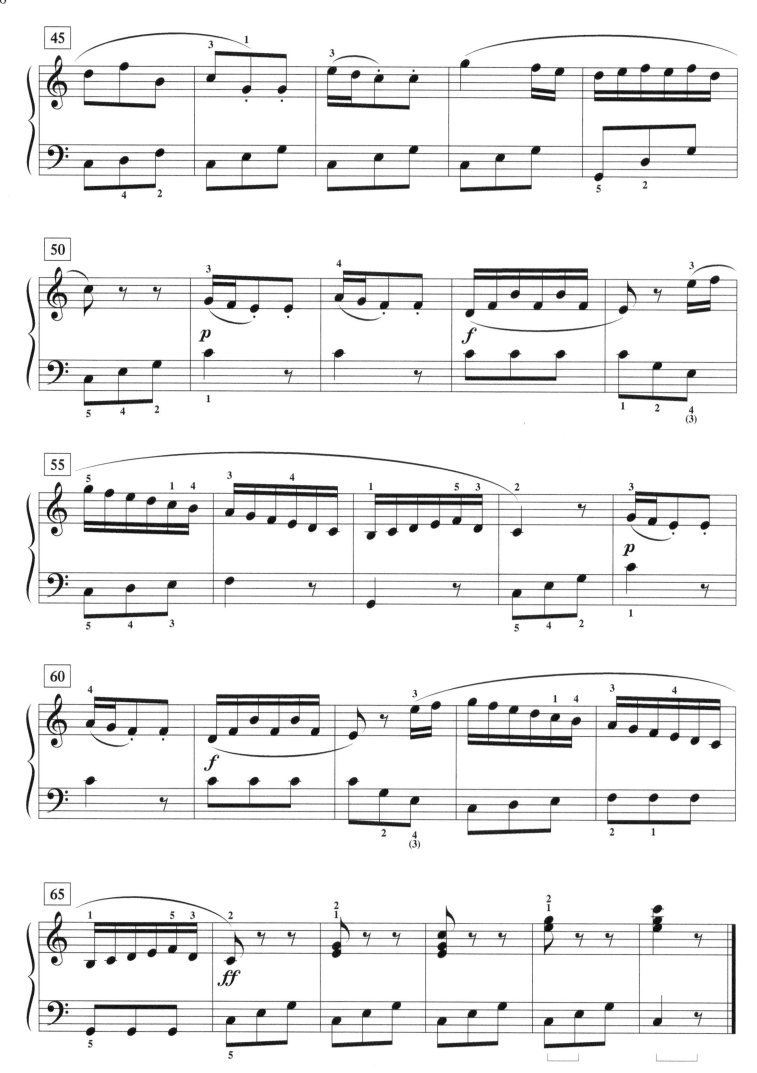

Sonatina in G Major
(Opus 168, No. 2)
1st Movement

Anton Diabelli
(1781–1858)

Teacher Part

Rondo for Four Hands
(Opus 163, No. 6)
Secondo

Anton Diabelli
(1781–1858)

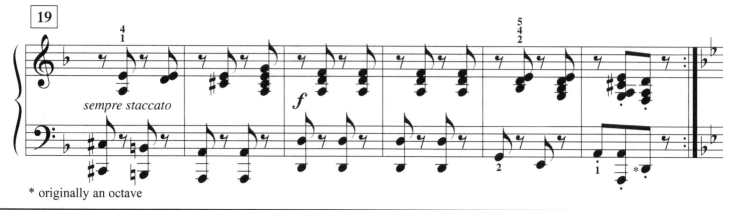

* originally an octave

Student Part

Rondo for Four Hands
(Opus 163, No. 6)
Primo

Anton Diabelli
(1781–1858)

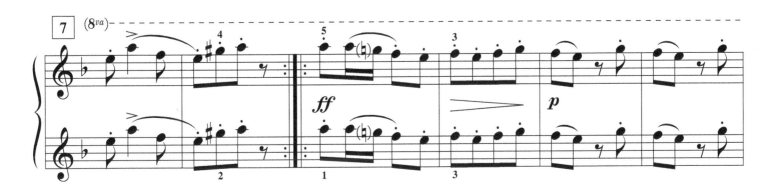

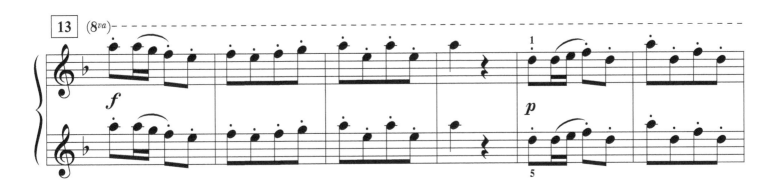

Secondo

Primo

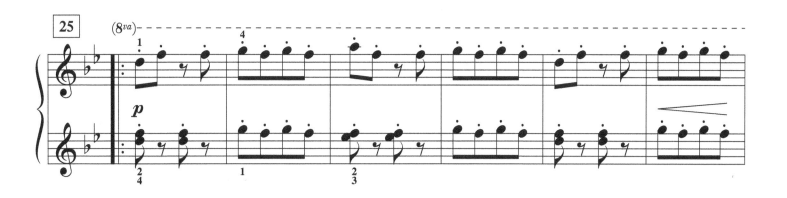

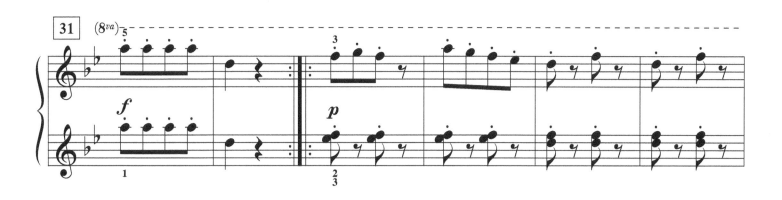

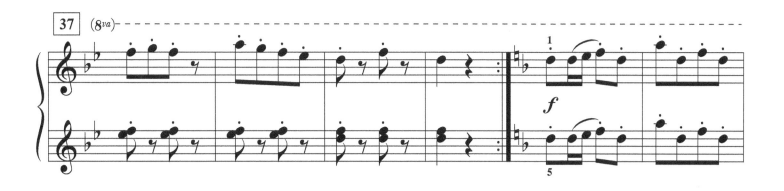

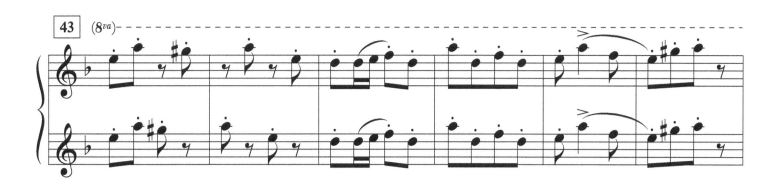

44

Primo

Two German Dances

I

Ludwig van Beethoven
(1770–1827)

II

Allegro in A Major

Leopold Mozart
(1719–1787)

Allegro moderato

A Little Flower
(Opus 205, No. 11)

Cornelius Gurlitt
(1820–1901)

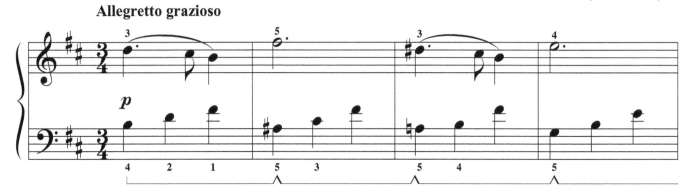

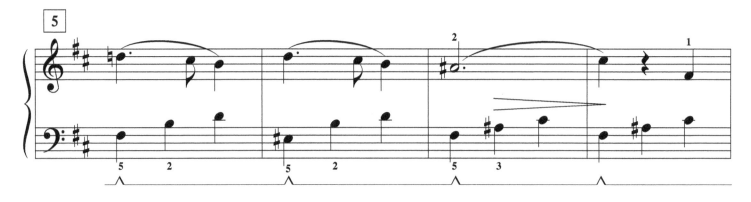

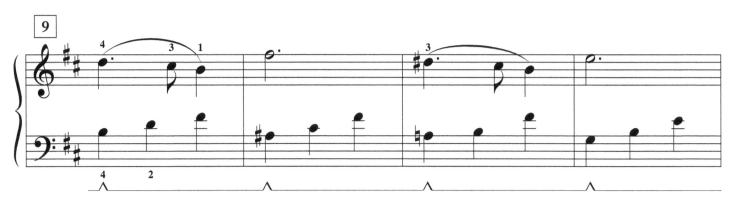

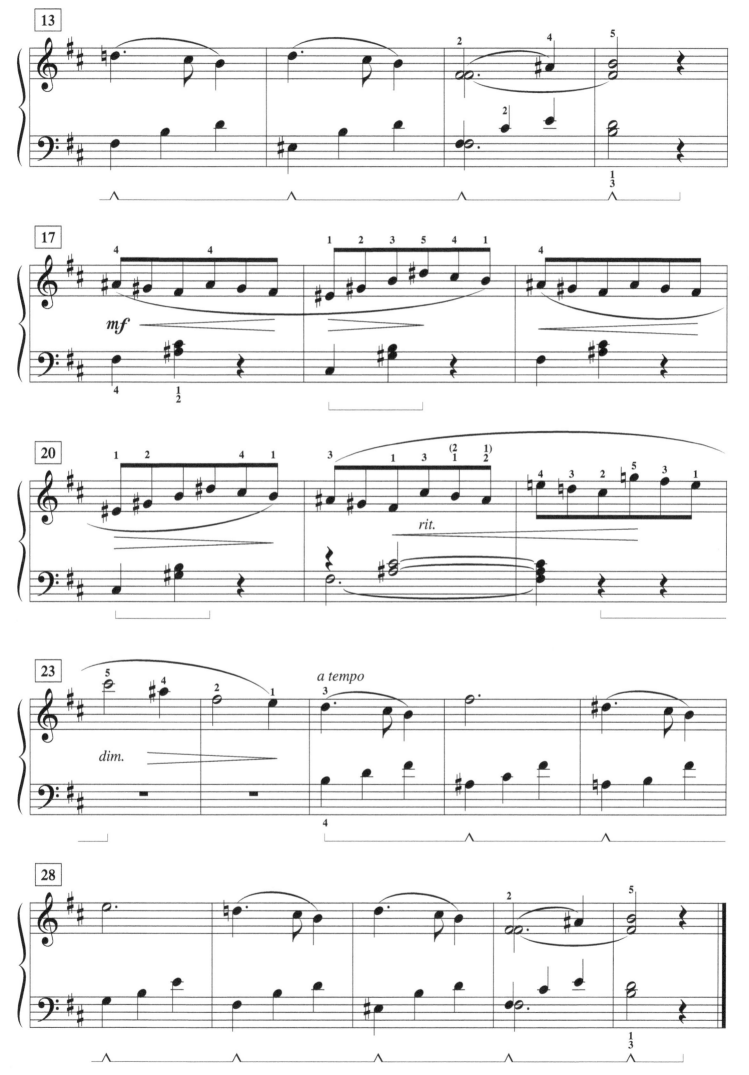

Arabesque
(Opus 100, No. 2)

Johann Friedrich Burgmüller
(1806–1874)

Allegro scherzando

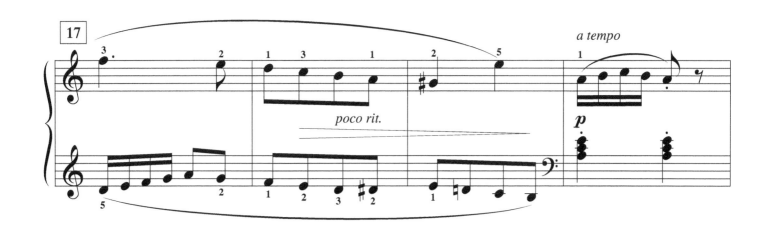

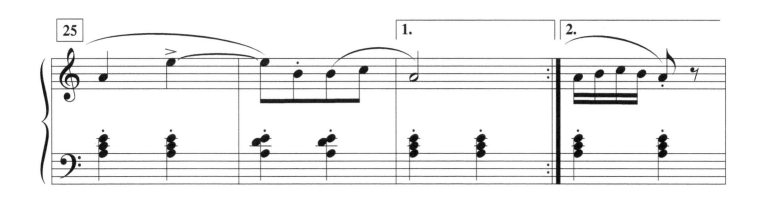

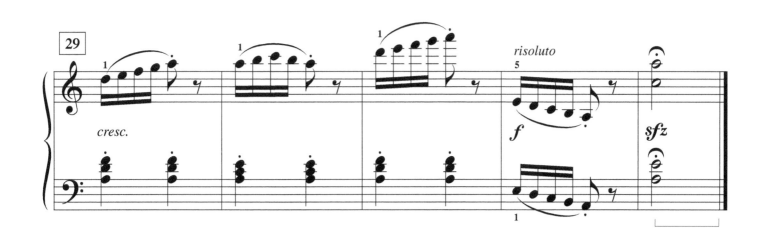

Ballade
(Opus 100, No. 15)

Johann Friedrich Burgmüller
(1806–1874)

Harmony of the Angels
(Opus 100, No. 21)

Johann Friedrich Burgmüller
(1806–1874)

Wild Rider
from Album for the Young
(Opus 68, No. 8)

Robert Schumann
(1810–1856)

Melody
from Album for the Young
(Opus 68, No. 1)

Robert Schumann
(1810–1856)

Spinning Song
(Opus 14, No. 4)

Albert Ellmenreich
(1816–1905)

Avalanche
(Opus 45, No. 2)

Stephen Heller
(1813–1888)

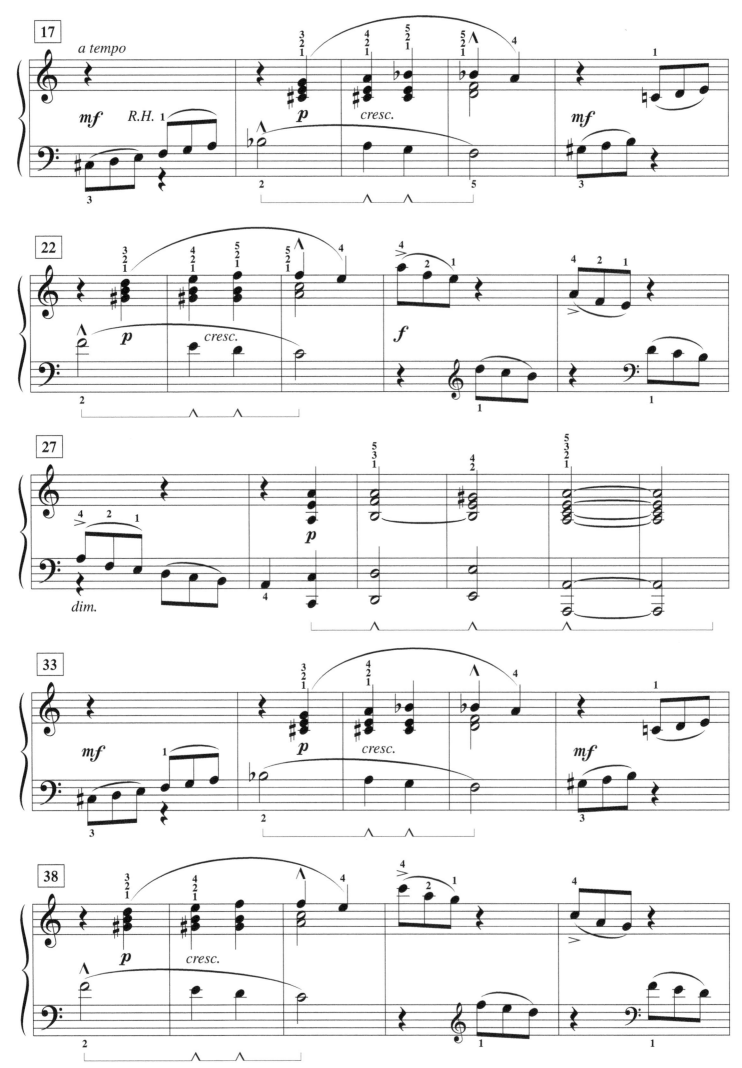

Gavotte
(from Opus 183, No. 1)

Carl Reinecke
(1824–1910)

Musette

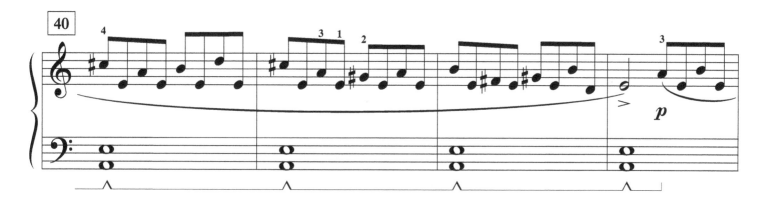

Contemporary
circa 1900 – present

Chinese Figurine
(from Christmas Gifts, No. 13)

Vladimir Rebikov
(1866–1920)

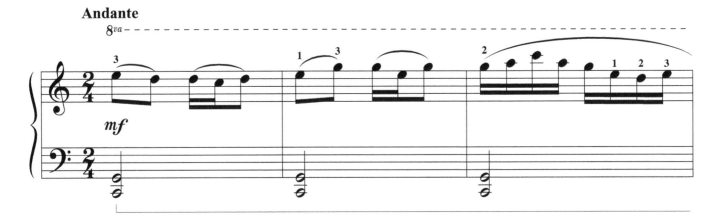

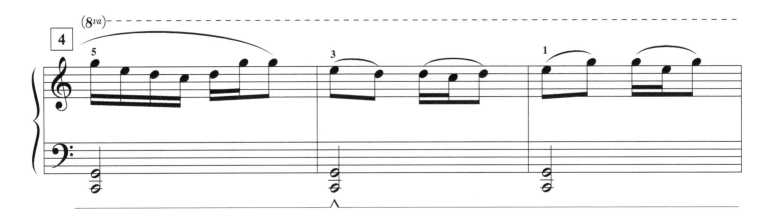

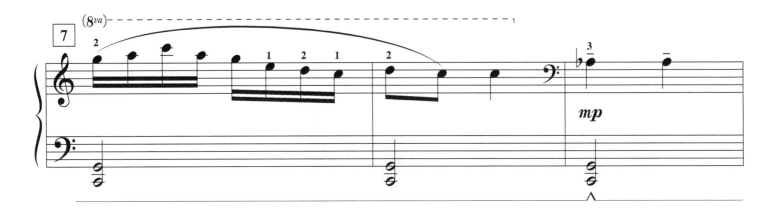

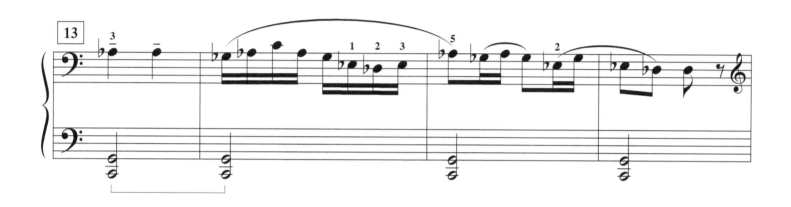

Playing Soldiers
(Opus 31, No. 4)

Vladimir Rebikov
(1866–1920)

Tempo di Marcia (♩ = 116)

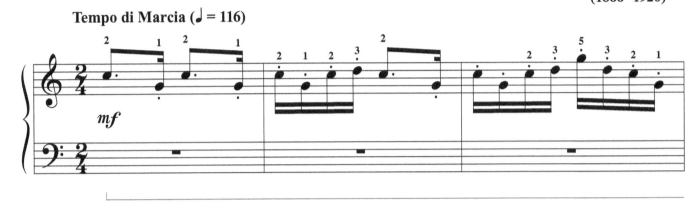

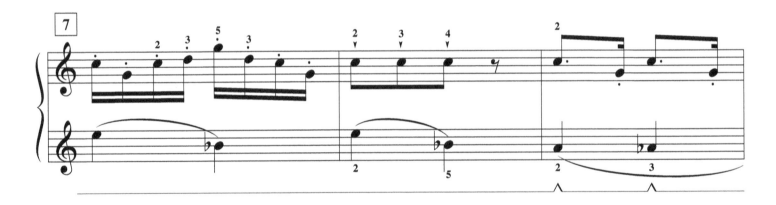

a) Play the L.H. over the R.H., closer to the fallboard.
b) Play the L.H. G staccato so the R.H. G may sound.

The Moons of Jupiter

Nancy Faber
(1955–)

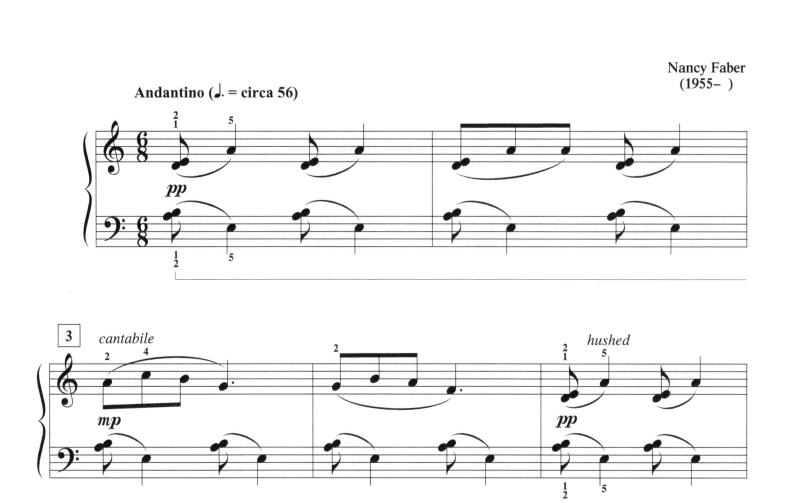

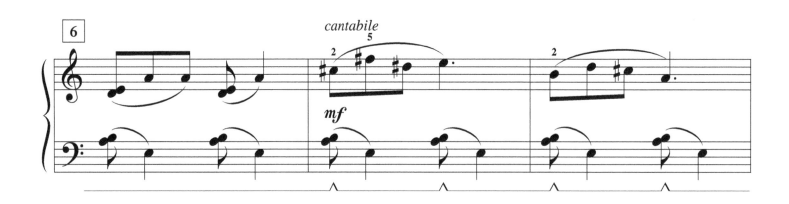

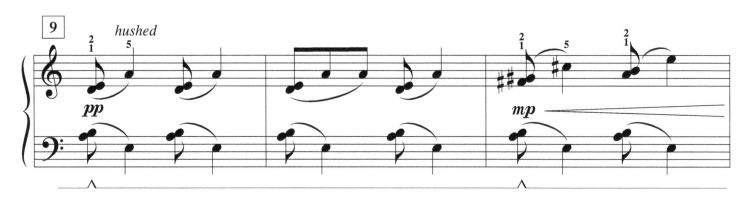

Song of the Range Rider
(from *Sagebrush Country, No. 1*)

George Frederick McKay
(1899–1970)

Cowboy Song
(from Sagebrush Country, No. 9)

George Frederick McKay
(1899–1970)

Sonatina

Russell Jacoby
(1955–)

Briskly, spirited

ALPHABETICAL INDEX OF TITLES

ALLEGRO in A Major . . . . L. Mozart 48

ALLEGRO in F Major . . . . Haydn .28

ARABESQUE (Op. 100, No.2) . . . . Burgmüller 52

AVALANCHE (Op. 45, No. 2) . . . . Heller 67

BALLADE (Op. 100, No. 15) . . . . Burgmüller 54

CHINESE FIGURINE (*Christmas Gifts*, No. 13) . . . . Rebikov 72

COWBOY SONG (*Sagebrush Country*, No. 9) . . . . McKay 80

FANFARE in C Major . . . . Duncombe 8

GAVOTTE (from Op. 183, No. 1) . . . . Reinecke 70

GERMAN DANCE in D Major . . . . Beethoven 46

GERMAN DANCE in D Major . . . . Beethoven 47

GERMAN DANCE in D Major . . . . Haydn 26

HARMONY OF THE ANGELS (Op. 100, No. 21) . . . . Burgmüller 57

A LITTLE FLOWER (Op. 205, No. 11) . . . . Gurlitt 50

MARCH in D Major (Anna Magdalena Bach Notebook) . . . . C.P.E. Bach 16

MELODY (*Album for the Young*, Op. 68, No. 1) . . . . Schumann 62

MINUET in A Minor . . . . Krieger 6

MINUET in D Minor . . . . Lully .9

MINUET in G Major . . . . Haydn 27

MINUET in G Major (Anna Magdalena Bach Notebook) 12

MINUET in G Minor (Anna Magdalena Bach Notebook) . . . . Pezold 14

THE MOONS OF JUPITER . . . . Faber 76

MUSETTE in D Major (Anna Magdalena Bach Notebook) 10

PLAYING SOLDIERS (Op. 31, No. 4) . . . . Rebikov 74

RONDO for Four Hands (Op. 163, No. 6) . . . . Diabelli 40

SOLFEGGIO in D Major . . . . J.C. Bach 18

SONATINA . . . . Jacoby 82

SONATINA in C Major (Op. 36, No. 1) . . . . Clementi 30

SONATINA in C Major . . . . Haslinger 22

SONATINA in G Major, 1st Mvt. (Op. 168, No. 2) . . . . Diabelli 37

SONG OF THE RANGE RIDER (*Sagebrush Country*, No. 1) . . . . . . McKay 78

SPINNING SONG (Op. 14, No. 4) . . . . Ellmenreich 64

TAMBOURIN . . . . Gossec 20

WILD RIDER (*Album for the Young*, Op. 68, No. 8) . . . . Schumann 60

FF1056

DICTIONARY OF MUSICAL TERMS

DYNAMIC MARKS

pp	*p*	*mp*	*mf*	*f*	*ff*
pianissimo	*piano*	*mezzo piano*	*mezzo forte*	*forte*	*fortissimo*
very soft	soft	moderately soft	moderately loud	loud	very loud

crescendo (cresc.)

Play gradually louder.

diminuendo (dim.) or decrescendo (decresc.)

Play gradually softer.

TEMPO MARKS

Adagio	*Andante*	*Moderato*	*Allegretto*	*Allegro*	*Vivace*
slowly	"walking speed" (slower than *Moderato*)	moderate tempo	rather fast	fast and lively	very fast

SIGN	TERM	DEFINITION
	a tempo	Return to the beginning tempo (speed).
accel.	*accelerando*	Gradually play faster.
	accent	Play this note louder.
	alla breve	Cut time. Short for $\frac{2}{2}$ time signature. The half note gets the beat. (Two half note beats per measure.)
	allegro moderato	Moderately fast.
	andantino	A tempo that is a bit faster than *andante*.
	appoggiatura	An ornament that looks like a grace note, but is played on the beat and shares the duration of the principal note. An appoggiatura resolves a dissonance to a consonance.
	armonioso	Harmoniously; with beautiful harmony.
	con brio	With spirit.
	D.C. al Fine	*Da Capo al Fine*. Return to the beginning and play until *Fine* (end).
	dolce	Sweetly.
	e	And (Italian). For example, *cresc. e rit.*
espr.	*espressivo*	Expressively.
	fermata	Hold this note longer than usual.
	gioviale	Jovially. (Cheerfully.)
	grazioso	Gracefully.
	legato	Smoothly, connected.

	leggiero	Light and nimble.
	lento	Slow; slower than *adagio*.
	marcato	Marked; each note well articulated.
	meno	Less. For example, *meno mosso* means "less motion."
	misterioso	Mysteriously.
	mosso	Motion.
	Notebook for Anna Magdalena Bach	A collection of pieces by J.S. Bach, his sons, and friends, presented to his wife Anna Magdalena as a gift.
Op.	**opus**	Work. A composer's compositions are often arranged in sequence, with each work given an *opus* number. Several pieces may be included in a single opus. Ex.: Op. 3, No. 1; Op. 3, No. 2, etc.
8va	*ottava*	Play one octave higher than written. When 8va is below the staff, play one octave lower.
	più	More. For example, *più cresc.* means more crescendo.
	poco	A little.
rall.	*rallentando*	Gradually slow down. Same as *ritardando*.
	risoluto	With firmness, decisiveness.
rit.	*ritardando*	Gradually slow down.
	ritenuto	Slowing of the tempo.
	ritmico	Rhythmically.
	scherzando	Playfully.
sfz or *sf*	*sforzando*	A sudden, strong accent.
	simile	Similarly. Continue in the same way. (Same pedaling, same use of staccato, etc.)
	slur	Connect the notes over or under a slur.
	sonatina	A little sonata.
	staccato	Play *staccato* notes detached, disconnected.
	subito	Suddenly. For example, *subito piano* means suddenly soft.
	tempo	The speed of the music.
	tempo di Marcia	March tempo.
	tenuto mark	Hold this note for its full value. Stress the note by pressing gently into the key.
tr	**trill**	A quick repetition of the principal note with the note above it. (The number and speed of the repetitions depend on the music.)

AUDIO TRACK INDEX

Track	Title	Composer	Page
1	MINUET in A Minor	Krieger	6
2	FANFARE in C Major	Duncombe	8
3	MINUET in D Minor	Lully	9
4	MUSETTE in D Major (Anna Magdalena Bach Notebook)		10
5	MINUET in G Major (Anna Magdalena Bach Notebook)		12
6	MINUET in G Minor (Anna Magdalena Bach Notebook)	Pezold	14
7	MARCH in D Major (Anna Magdalena Bach Notebook)	C.P.E. Bach	16
8	SOLFEGGIO in D Major	J.C. Bach	18
9	TAMBOURIN	Gossec	20
10-11	SONATINA in C Major	Haslinger	22
12	GERMAN DANCE in D Major	Haydn	26
13	MINUET in G Major	Haydn	27
14	ALLEGRO in F Major	Haydn	28
15-17	SONATINA in C Major (Op. 36, No. 1)	Clementi	30
18	SONATINA in G Major, 1st Mvt. (Op. 168, No. 2)	Diabelli	37
19	RONDO for Four Hands (Op. 163, No. 6)	Diabelli	40
20	GERMAN DANCE in D Major (I)	Beethoven	46
21	GERMAN DANCE in D Major (II)	Beethoven	47
22	ALLEGRO in A Major	L. Mozart	48
23	A LITTLE FLOWER (Op. 205, No. 11)	Gurlitt	50
24	ARABESQUE (Op. 100, No.2)	Burgmüller	52
25	BALLADE (Op. 100, No. 15)	Burgmüller	54
26	HARMONY OF THE ANGELS (Op. 100, No. 21)	Burgmüller	57
27	WILD RIDER (*Album for the Young*, Op. 68, No. 8)	Schumann	60
28	MELODY (*Album for the Young*, Op. 68, No. 1)	Schumann	62
29	SPINNING SONG (Op. 14, No. 4)	Ellmenreich	64
30	AVALANCHE (Op. 45, No. 2)	Heller	67
31	GAVOTTE (from Op. 183, No. 1)	Reinecke	70
32	CHINESE FIGURINE (*Christmas Gifts*, No. 13)	Rebikov	72
33	PLAYING SOLDIERS (Op. 31, No. 4)	Rebikov	74
34	THE MOONS OF JUPITER	Faber	76
35	SONG OF THE RANGE RIDER (*Sagebrush Country*, No. 1)	McKay	78
36	COWBOY SONG (*Sagebrush Country*, No. 9)	McKay	80
37	SONATINA	Jacoby	82